CW01432263

50 Unique Wedding Readings
Including Wedding Poems, Wedding Blessings and Non-Religious Writings.

Marie Kay

Copyright © 2015 Marie Kay

All rights reserved.

ISBN:
ISBN-13:
978-1511773164

ISBN-10:
1511773162

TO MY HUSBAND

I can hardly put in words, how much you matter.

CONTENTS

Forward
WHAT'S IN A READING?

So what's the point of a reading anyway? At the typical wedding ceremony, you have a procession, a greeting, a song, a reading, an Officiant's message, vows, and joila'. Is the reading just something to kill time? An interlude for the musician to set-up? A chance to think about romance and commitment for just another moment? Perhaps all of the above. But if you're looking to set a particular tone in your ceremony, it's as important as music.

What's the aim of your wedding, in terms of what it means to you, your guests, your attendants? What's your personal style? Humorous? Religious? Ironic? Poetic? Lyrical?

There are few adults, in the U.S. at least, who haven't heard the common Corinthians reading, at many, many, (*too many)* weddings. And while each bride and groom likely thought, "Our wedding will be unique," well, doing the same thing the same way, is counter to that aim.

So put on your romance hats and see if there's an unexpected reading that might offer your betrothed – and your guests – a pleasant surprise. Read on, and imagine the creative possibilities! There are historical love letters, song lyrics, poems, even an Aesop's fable! With any luck, you'll have those at your wedding emotionally stirred and actually remembering your choice. Or at least questioning…How did you pick that beautiful reading?

Biblical Readings
#1 - #7

Ruth 1, 16-17

Where you go I will go, and where you stay I will stay. Your people will be my people and your god my God. Where you die I will die, and there I will be burred. May the Lord deal with me, be it ever so severely, if anything but death separates you and me.

Ecclesiastes 4

Two are better than one, because they have a good return for their work: If one falls down, his friend can help him up. But pity the man who falls and has no one to help him up!

Also, if two lie down together, they will keep warm. But how can one keep warm alone? Though one may be overpowered, two can defend themselves. A cord of three strands is not quickly broken.

Genesis 2:18-24

The LORD God said, "It is not good for the man to be alone. I will make a helper suitable for him." Now the LORD God had formed out of the ground all the beasts of the field and all the birds of the air. He brought them to the man to see what he would name them; and whatever the man called each living creature, that was its name. So the man gave names to all the livestock, the birds of the air and all the beasts of the field. But for Adam no suitable helper was found. So the LORD God caused the man to fall into a deep sleep; and while he was sleeping, he took one of the man's ribs and closed up the place with flesh. Then the LORD God made a woman from the rib he had taken out of the man, and he brought her to the man.

The man said, "This is now bone of my bones and flesh of my flesh; she shall be called 'woman,' for she was taken out of man." For this reason a man will leave his father and mother and be united to his wife, and they will become one flesh.

Romans 12: 9-21

Love must be sincere. Hate what is evil; cling to what is good. Be devoted to one another in brotherly love. Honor one another above yourselves. Never be lacking in zeal, but keep your spiritual fervor, serving the Lord. Be joyful in hope, patient in affliction, faithful in prayer. Share with God's people who are in need. Practice hospitality. Bless those who persecute you; bless and do not curse. Rejoice with those who rejoice; mourn with those who mourn. Live in harmony with one another. Do not be proud, but be willing to associate with people of low position. Do not be conceited. Do not repay anyone evil for evil. Be careful to do what is right in the eyes of everybody. If it is possible, as far as it depends on you, live at peace with everyone.

Colossians 3:12-17

Therefore, as God's chosen people, holy and dearly loved, clothe yourselves with compassion, kindness, humility, gentleness and patience. Bear with each other and forgive whatever grievances you may have against one another. Forgive as the Lord forgave you. And over all these virtues put on love, which binds them all together in perfect unity. Let the peace of Christ rule in your hearts, since as members of one body you were called to peace. And be thankful. Let the word of Christ dwell in you richly as you teach and admonish one another with all wisdom, and as you sing psalms, hymns and spiritual songs with gratitude in your hearts to God. And whatever you do, whether in word or deed, do it all in the name of the Lord Jesus, giving thanks to God the Father through him.

Ephesians 5:24-33

Husbands, love your wives, just as Christ loved the church and gave himself up for her to make her holy, cleansing her by the washing with water through the word, and to present her to himself as a radiant church, without stain or wrinkle or any other blemish, but holy and blameless. In this same way, husbands ought to love their wives as their own bodies. He who loves his wife loves himself. After all, no one ever hated his own body, but he feeds and cares for it, just as Christ does the church- for we are members of his body. "For this reason a man will leave his father and mother and be united to his wife, and the two will become one flesh." This is a profound mystery-but I am talking about Christ and the church. However, each one of you also must love his wife as he loves himself, and the wife must respect her husband.

And, while it's the most commonly used, it bears inclusion, just in case:

I Corinthians 13:4-13

Love is patient and kind; love does not envy or boast; it is not arrogant or rude. It does not insist on its own way; it is not irritable or resentful; it does not rejoice at wrongdoing, but rejoices with the truth. Love bears all things, believes all things, hopes all things, endures all things.

Love never ends. As for prophecies, they will pass away; as for tongues, they will cease; as for knowledge, it will pass away. For we know in part and we prophesy in part, but when the perfect comes, the partial will pass away. When I was a child, I spoke like a child, I thought like a child, I reasoned like a child. When I became a man, I gave up childish ways. For now we see in a mirror dimly, but then face to face. Now I know in part; then I shall know fully, even as I have been fully known.

So now faith, hope, and love abide, these three; but the greatest of these is love.

From Hymns
Readings #8- #10

Here's an original idea...take the lyrics of a classic hymn, and you'll find the notion of "love" as a universal thing; a prayer that is as relevant to one's life-love, as it is to one's God-love. And doing this, would be an original and creative choice for a wedding, certainly. With a less-common hymn, the tune won't necessarily even be imagined, just the poetry of it.

Take My Life and Let It Be, by Francis R. Havergal, 1874

Take my hands, and let them move
At the impulse of Thy love;
Take my feet, and let them be
Swift and beautiful for Thee.
Swift and beautiful for Thee.
Take my voice, and let me sing
Always, only, for my King;
Take my lips, and let them be
Filled with messages from Thee.
Filled with messages from Thee.
Take my silver and my gold:
Not a mite would I withhold;
Take my intellect, and use
Ev'ry pow'r as Thou shalt choose.
Ev'ry pow'r as Thou shalt choose.
Take my will, and make it Thine,
It shall be no longer mine;
Take my heart, it is Thine own,
It shall be Thy royal throne.
It shall be Thy royal throne.
Take my love, my Lord, I pour
At Thy feet its treasure store;
Take myself, and I will be,
Ever, only, all for Thee.
Ever, only, all for Thee.

Blessed Be The Tie That Binds, John Fawcett, 1775

Blessed be the tie that binds
Our hearts in Christian love;
The fellowship of kindred minds
Is like that to that above.

Before our Father's throne
We pour our ardent prayers;
Our fears, our hopes, our aims are one
Our comforts and our cares.

We share each other's woes,
Our mutual burdens bear;
And often for each other flows
The sympathizing tear.

When we asunder part,
It gives us inward pain;
But we shall still be joined in heart,
And hope to meet again.

This glorious hope revives
Our courage by the way;
While each in expectation lives,
And longs to see the day.

From sorrow, toil and pain,
And sin, we shall be free,
And perfect love and friendship reign
Through all eternity

Be Thou My Vision (by Dallan Forgaill, Ancient Irish, to English Mary E. Byrne)

Be Thou my Vision, O Lord of my heart;
Naught be all else to me, save that Thou art
Thou my best Thought, by day or by night,
Waking or sleeping, Thy presence my light.

Be Thou my Wisdom, and Thou my true Word;
I ever with Thee and Thou with me, Lord;
Thou my great Father, I Thy true son;
Thou in me dwelling, and I with Thee one.

Be Thou my battle Shield, Sword for the fight;
Be Thou my Dignity, Thou my Delight;
Thou my soul's Shelter, Thou my high Tower:
Raise Thou me heavenward, O Power of my power.

From Stage Musicals
Readings #11 - #12

Show Boat, (the Edna Ferber novel which the show was based on), 1926

Wasn't marriage, like life, unstimulating and unprofitable and somewhat empty when too well-ordered and protected and guarded? Wasn't it finer, more splendid, more nourishing, when it was, like life itself, a mixture of the sordid and the magnificent; of mud and stars; of earth and flowers; of love and hate and laughter and tears and ugliness and beauty and hurt?

From HMS Pinafore, by Gilbert & Sullivan 1878

Oh joy, oh rapture unforeseen,
The clouded sky is now serene,
The god of day — the orb of love,
Has hung his ensign high above,
The sky is all ablaze.
With wooing words and loving song
We'll chase the lagging hours along,
And if he finds the maiden coy,
We'll murmur forth decorous joy
In dreamy roundelays
....I shall marry with a wife,
In my humble rank of life!
And you, my own, are she.
I must wander to and fro;
But wherever I may go,
I shall never be untrue to thee!

Shakespeare, in small doses.
Readings #13 - #16

No one can out-write him. Use a long passage, or consider sampling from a couple of the shorter ones. Prose and poetry seem one and the same with these sentiments.

Use the following two passages together, for complimentary quotes in a single reading:

From Hamlet:
Doubt thou the stars are fire;
Doubt that the sun doth move;
Doubt truth to be a liar:
But never doubt I love.

Romeo and Juliet
My bounty is as boundless as the sea,
My love as deep; the more I give to thee,
The more I have, for both are infinite.

Sonnet 116

Let me not to the marriage of true minds
Admit impediments. Love is not love
Which alters when it alteration finds,
Or bends with the remover to remove:
O no! it is an ever-fixed mark
That looks on tempests and is never shaken;
It is the star to every wandering bark,
Whose worth's unknown, although his height be taken.
Love's not Time's fool, though rosy lips and cheeks
Within his bending sickle's compass come:
Love alters not with his brief hours and weeks,
But bears it out even to the edge of doom.
If this be error and upon me proved,
I never writ, nor no man ever loved.

Sonnet 18

Shall I compare thee to a summer's day?
Thou art more lovely and more temperate:
Rough winds do shake the darling buds of May,
And summer's lease hath all too short a date:
Sometime too hot the eye of heaven shines,
And often is his gold complexion dimm'd;
And every fair from fair sometime declines,
By chance or nature's changing course untrimm'd;
But thy eternal summer shall not fade
Nor lose possession of that fair thou owest;
Nor shall Death brag thou wander'st in his shade,
When in eternal lines to time thou growest:
> *So long as men can breathe or eyes can see,*
> *So long lives this and this gives life to thee.*

<u>Loves Labours Lost:</u>

But love, first learned in a lady's eyes,
Lives not alone immured in the brain;
But, with the motion of all elements,
Courses as swift as thought in every power,
And gives to every power a double power,
Above their functions and their offices.
It adds a precious seeing to the eye;
A lover's eyes will gaze an eagle blind;
A lover's ear will hear the lowest sound,
When the suspicious head of theft is stopp'd:
Love's feeling is more soft and sensible
Than are the tender horns of cockl'd snails;
Love's tongue proves dainty Bacchus
  gross in taste:

For valour, is not Love a Hercules,
Still climbing trees in the Hesperides?
Subtle as Sphinx; as sweet and musical
As bright Apollo's lute, strung with his hair:
And when Love speaks, the voice of all the gods
Makes heaven drowsy with the harmony.
Loves Labours Lost

Traditional Prayers & Blessings
Readings #17 - #22

<u>Apache Blessing</u>

Now you will feel no rain, for each of you will be shelter for the other.

Now you will feel no cold, for each of you will be warmth for the other.

Now there is no more loneliness, for each of you will be companion for the other.

Now you are two persons, but there is only one life before you.

Go now to your dwelling place to begin the days of your life together.

May your days together be good and long upon the earth.

Note how similar the previous is to the following:

Salish Marriage Blessing

Now for you there is no rain, for one is shelter to the other.
Now for you the sun shall not burn, for one is shelter to the other.
Now for you nothing is hard or bad, for the hardness and badness is taken by one for the other.
Now for you there is no night, for one is light to the other,
Now for you the snow has ended always, for one is protection for the other.
It is that way, from now on, from now on. And now there is comfort.
Now there is no loneliness. Now forever, forever, there is no loneliness.

Olde Irish Blessing

May the road rise to meet you,
May the wind be always at your back.
May the sun shine warm upon your face,
The rains fall soft upon your fields.
And until we meet again,
May God hold you in the palm of his hand.

Irish Wedding Prayer by Robert Louis Stevenson

Lord, behold our family here assembled.
We thank you for this place in which we dwell,
for the love that unites us,
for the peace accorded us this day,
for the hope with which we expect the morrow,
for the health, the work, the food,
and the bright skies that make our lives delightful;
for our friends in all parts of the earth.
Amen

From Mother Theresa:
*Spread love everywhere you go: first of all in your own
house.
Give love to your children, to your wife or husband, to a
next door neighbor...
Let no one ever come to you without leaving better and
happier.
Be the living expression of God's kindness;
kindness in your face, kindness in your eyes, kindness in
your smile,
kindness in your warm greeting.*

THE PRAYER, By St. Francis of Assisi

Lord, make us instruments of your peace.
Where there is hatred, let us sow love;
Where there is injury, pardon;
Where there is discord, union;
Where there is doubt, faith;
Where there is despair, hope;
Where there is darkness, light;
Where there is sadness, joy;
O Divine Master, Grant that we may not so much seek
To be consoled as to console,
To be understood as to understand,
To be loved as to love.
For it is in giving that we receive;
It is in pardoning that we are pardoned;
And it is in dying that we are born to eternal life.
Amen

Tell everyone around you of the great love of
God. When all else fails, use words. "
-St. Francis

From The Buddha
Readings #23 - #25

One should be honest and faithful, without deception, ranting, hinting or belittling, not always quick to add gain to gain, but with the temptations guarded, moderate in food, a peacemaker, observant, active and hard-working, a mediator, mindful, with proper conversation, steady-going, resolute and sensible, not craving sensory pleasures, but mindful and prudent. This is the unsurpassed teaching concerning a person's proper ethical conduct. — Buddha

One who is wise and disciplined,
Always kindly and intelligent,
Humble and free from pride --
One like this will win respect.
　　　Rising early and scorning laziness,
Remaining calm in moments of strife,
faultless in conduct and clever in actions --
One like this will win respect.
　　　Being able to make and keep friends,
Welcoming others and sharing with them,
A guide, philosopher and friend --
One like this will win respect.
　　　Being generous and kind in speech
Doing good for others
And treating all alike --
one like this will win respect.
　　　-- Buddha

One could end the previous with a directive of
your own, such as:
　　　So do all this, to respect one another.

If beings knew as I know the results of sharing gifts, they would not enjoy their use without sharing them with others. Now, would the taint of stinginess obsess the heart and stay there? Even if it were their last and final bit of food, they would not enjoy its use without sharing it, if there were anyone to receive it. "

- Buddha

Classic Poems for Weddings
Readings #26 - #29

"Love's Philosophy" Percy Bysshe Shelley (1792-1822)

The fountains mingle with the rivers
And the rivers with the oceans,
The winds of heaven mix forever
With a sweet emotion;
Nothing in the world is single;
All things by law divine
In one spirit meet and mingle.
Why not I with thine?

See the mountains kiss high heaven
And the waves clasp one another;
No sister-flower would be forgiven
If it disdained its brother,
And the sunlight clasps the earth
And the moonbeams kiss the sea:
What is all this sweet work worth
If thou kiss not me?

Love and Harmony by William Blake

Love and harmony combine,
And round our souls entwine
While thy branches mix with mine,
And our roots together join.
        Joys upon our branches sit,
Chirping loud and singing sweet;
Like gentle streams beneath our feet
Innocence and virtue meet.
        Thou the golden fruit dost bear,
I am clad in flowers fair;
Thy sweet boughs perfume the air,
And the turtle buildeth there.
        There she sits and feeds her young,
Sweet I hear her mournful song;
And thy lovely leaves among,
There is love, I hear his tongue.
        There his charming nest doth lay,
        There he sleeps the night away;
There he sports along the day,
And doth among our branches play.

"Surrender" by Emily Dickinson

Doubt me, my dim companion!
Why, God would be content
With but a fraction of the love
Poured thee without a stint.

The whole of me, forever,
What more the woman can, --
Say quick, that I may dower thee
With last delight I own!

It cannot be my spirit,
For that was thine before;
I ceded all of dust I knew, --
What opulence the more

Had I, a humble maiden,
Whose farthest of degree
Was that she might,
Some distant heaven,
Dwell timidly with thee!

"The Passionate Shepherd to His Love"
by Christopher Marlowe (1590s)

Come live with me and be my love,
And we will all the pleasures prove
That hills and valleys, dale and field,
And all the craggy mountains yield.
There will we sit upon the rocks,
And see the shepherds feed their flocks,
By shallow rivers to whose falls
Melodious birds sing madrigals.
There I will make thee beds of roses
And a thousand fragrant posies,
A cap of flowers, and a kirtle
Embroider'd all with leaves of myrtle;
A gown made of the finest wool
Which from our pretty lambs we pull;
Fair linèd slippers for the cold,
With buckles of the purest gold;
A belt of straw and ivy buds,
With coral clasps and amber studs;
And if these pleasures may thee move,
Come live with me, and be my love.
Thy silver dishes for thy meat
As precious as the gods do eat,
Shall on an ivory table be
Prepared each day for thee and me.
The shepherd swains shall dance and sing
For thy delight each May-morning:
If these delights thy mind may move,
Then live with me and be my love.

* For more uses of poetry in wedding vows, see:
New & Traditional Wedding Vow Examples
+ 10 Methods to Write Your Own.

Classic Writings, Novels & Essays
Readings #30 - #36

From "The Prophet" by Kahlil Gibran
Let there be spaces in your togetherness,
And let the winds of heavens dance between you.

Love one another, but make not a bond of love:
Let it rather be a moving sea between the shores of your
souls.

Fill each other's cup but drink not from one cup.
Give one another of your bread but eat not from the
same loaf.

Sing and dance together and be joyous, but let each
one of you be alone,

Even as the strings of a lute are alone though they
quiver with the same music.

Give your hearts, but not into each other's keeping.
For only the hand of Life can contain your hearts.
And stand together yet not too near together:
For the pillars of the temple stand apart,
And the oak tree and the cypress grow not in each
other's shadow.

From George Eliot (Mary Ann Evans) 1819-1880

Oh, the comfort, the inexpressible comfort of feeling safe with a person, having neither to weigh thoughts nor measure words, but pouring them all out, just as they are, chaff and grain together, certain that a faithful hand will take and sift them, keep what is worth keeping, and with a breath of kindness blow the rest away.

Select Quotes from Henry David Thoreau (1817-1862)

"There is no remedy for love, but to love more."

"What lies behind us and what lies ahead of us are tiny matters compared to what lives within us."

"Friends... they cherish one another's hopes. They are kind to one another's dreams."

"I learned this, at least, by my experiment: that if one advances confidently in the direction of his dreams, and endeavors to live the life which he has imagined, he will meet with a success unexpected in common hours."

"Let go of the past and go for the future. Go confidently in the direction of your dreams. Live the life you imagined."

From "Persuasion" by Jane Austen (1775-1817):

Dare not say that man forgets sooner than woman, that his love has an earlier death. I have loved none but you. Unjust I may have been, weak and resentful I have been, but never inconstant. You alone have brought me to Bath. For you alone, I think and plan. Have you not seen this? Can you fail to have understood my wishes? I had not waited even these ten days, could I have read your feelings, as I think you must have penetrated mine. I can hardly write. I am every instant hearing something which overpowers me. You sink your voice, but I can distinguish the tones of that voice when they would be lost on others. Too good, too excellent creature! You do us justice, indeed. You do believe that there is true attachment and constancy among men. Believe it to be most fervent, most undeviating, in F. W.

What is a successful marriage but the greatest friendship?

Great Quotes on Friendship:
*"Don't walk in front of me, I may not follow.
Don't walk behind me, I may not lead.
Just walk beside me and be my friend."*
- Albert Camus (1913-1960)

*Friendship improves happiness, and abates
misery, by doubling our joys, and dividing our grief.* -
Joseph Addison and alternatively attributed to a Swedish
proverb.

*The glory of friendship is not the outstretched
hand, nor the kindly smile, nor the joy of
companionship; it is the spiritual inspiration that comes
to one when he discovers that someone else believes in
him and is willing to trust him with his friendship.*
-- Ralph Waldo Emerson

*"And a youth said, Speak to us of Friendship,
and he answered saying:
Your friend is your needs answered. He is your
field which you sow with love and reap with
thanksgiving. And he is your board and your fireside.
For you come to him with your hunger, and you seek him
for peace."*
-- Kahlil Gibran

Song Lyrics
Readings #37 - #38

Song lyrics don't exclusively succeed inside of a tune.

Sometimes a song lyric will leave the listener with a sense of familiarity that's uplifting, yet without the complete realization it's even a song lyric they're hearing!

"All The World Will Be Jealous of Me"
Ernest Ball, Al Dubin, 1917

I was jealous and hurt
when your lips kissed a rose,
Or your eyes from my own chanced to stray:
I have tried all in vain
Many times to propose,
Now at last I've found courage to say;

Let's suppose that the lips I found kissing a rose
Were to tell me to look in your eyes,
If I'd find there a light that for me only glows
More and more would my heart realize;
The roses all envy the bloom on your cheek,
And the sun even envies your smile;
The birds in the wildwood are stifled when you speak,
Their songs don't seem half worth the while.

The light in your eyes makes the bright stars
grow pale,
They're jealous as jealous can be;
But when one word of sign tells them all you are mine,
all the world will be jealous of me.

And if you recognize this one, would it not bring a smile to every face?

<u>"I've Grown Accustomed To Her Face" Frederick Loewe & Alan Jay Lerner</u>

I've grown accustomed to her face.
She almost makes the day begin.
I've grown accustomed to the tune that
She whistles night and noon.
Her smiles, her frowns, Her ups, her downs
Are second nature to me now;
Like breathing out and breathing in.
I was serenely independent and content before we met;
Surely I could always be that way again- And yet
I've grown accustomed to her look;
Accustomed to her voice;
Accustomed to her face.
I'm so used to hear her say
"Good morning" every day.
Her joys, her woes,
Her highs, her lows,
Are second nature to me now;
Like breathing out and breathing in.
I'm very grateful she's a woman
And so easy to forget;
Rather like a habit
One can always break-
And yet,
I've grown accustomed to the trace
Of something in the air;
Accustomed to her face.

It Came From Hollywood
Readings #39 - #41

While they can't be printed here in full, because the studios own the script copyrights, this list may spark both your memory, and your imagination. Review the speeches in full, and you might be "sold" on a screenwriter's prose, for your big day. Nora Ephron, anyone? All movies available on Amazon.com for download.

Harry's New Year's Eve speech to Sally in *When Harry Met Sally...*

It's the speech that begins with, "*I love that you get cold when it's seventy-one degrees out. "I love that it takes you an hour and a half to order a sandwich...when you realize you want to spend the rest of your life with somebody, you want the rest of your life to start as soon as possible*." That speech.

The *Sleepless in Seattle* love speech by Tom Hanks' character, which starts with:

"It was a million tiny little things that, when you added them all up, they meant we were supposed to be together...and I knew it..."

From, *As Good As It Gets*, Jack Nicholson's big love speech. It's the one that includes:

"I think most people miss that about you...and I watch them...never get that they just met the greatest woman alive. And the fact that I get it makes me feel good, about me..."

Why not do a movie speech? Everyone gets a kick out of a heart-tugging movie moment that they can all remember.

Famous Love Letters
Readings #42 - #47

Let's consider the really unexpected; famous love letters! They're real, they've stood the test of time, and they're hardly typical. For the sake of timing in your ceremony, more than one love letter could be used. In the case of a largely recognizable author, you might save the reveal of who it is until *after* the reading, for a pleasant surprise of identity, to serve as the story's conclusion.

Katharine Mansfield (1888-1923) to
John Middleton Murray

My love for you tonight is so deep and tender that it seems to be outside myself as well. I am fast shut up like a little lake in the embrace of some big mountains. If you were to climb up the mountains, You would see me down below, deep and shining - and quite fathomless, my dear. You might drop your heart into me and you'd never hear it touch bottom. I love you – I love you.

From Victor Hugo (1802-1885) to Adele Foucher

When two souls, which have sought each other for, however long in the throng, have finally found each other ...a union, fiery and pure as they themselves are... begins on earth and continues forever in heaven.

This union is love, true love, ... a religion, which deifies the loved one, whose life comes from devotion and passion, and for which the greatest sacrifices are the sweetest delights.

This is the love which you inspire in me... Your soul is made to love with the purity and passion of angels; but perhaps it can only love another angel, in which case I must tremble with apprehension. Yours Forever.

Using a letter like this next, might require an introduction:

"The Love Letters Between Elizabeth Barret, and Robert Browning are some of the most touching expressions of mutual affection, and we share some with you now, as our couple shares their sentiments, so well-written, this way:"

From Robert Browning (1812-1889) to Elizabeth Barrett Browning:

...Would I, if I could, supplant one of any of the affections that I know to have taken root in you - that great and solemn one, for instance. I feel that if I could get myself remade, as if turned to gold, I would not even then desire to become more than the mere setting to that diamond you must always wear.

The regard and esteem you now give me, in this letter, and which I press to my heart and bow my head upon, is all I can take and all too embarrassing, using all my gratitude.

From Elizabeth Barrett Browning (1806-1861) to Robert Browning:

And now listen to me in turn. You have touched me more profoundly than I thought even you could have touched me - my heart was full when you came here today. Henceforward I am yours for everything....

From Jane Clairmont to Lord Byron -- 1815

You bid me write short to you and I have much to say. You also bade me believe that it was a fancy which made me cherish an attachment for you. It cannot be a fancy since you have been for the last year the object upon which every solitary moment led me to muse.

I do not expect you to love me, I am not worthy of your love. I feel you are superior, yet much to my surprise, more to my happiness, you betrayed passions I had believed no longer alive in your bosom.

Shall I also have to ruefully experience the want of happiness? Shall I reject it when it is offered? I may appear to you imprudent, vicious; my opinions detestable, my theory depraved; but one thing, at least, time shall show you: that I love gently and with affection, that I am incapable of anything approaching to the feeling of revenge or malice; I do assure you, your future will shall be mine, and everything you shall do or say, I shall not question.

Lovely. *"I do assure you, your future will shall be mine, and everything you shall do or say, I shall not question."* That excerpt could practically be a vow as well as a reading. Remember to, that it's your wedding, and you can shorten or take excerpts as you see fit. The authors...won't likely know.

From Abigail Adams (1744-1818) to John Adams

Well-known for their profound partnership and romance, during the United State's earliest days, over 1,000 of their personal letters have survived to present-day. This from one of Abigail's:

My Dearest Friend,

...Should I draw you the picture of my heart it would be what I hope you would still love though it contained nothing new. The early possession you obtained there, and the absolute power you have obtained over it, leaves not the smallest space unoccupied.

I look back to the early days of our acquaintance and friendship as to the days of love and innocence, and, with an indescribable pleasure, I have seen near a score of years roll over our heads with an affection heightened and improved by time, nor have the dreary years of absence in the smallest degree effaced from my mind the image of the dear untitled man to whom I gave my heart.

Another letter from Abigail to John:

...There is a tie more binding than Humanity, and stronger than Friendship ... unite these, and there is a threefold chord — and by this chord I am not ashamed to say that I am bound, nor do I [believe] that you are wholly free from it.

From Woodrow Wilson (1856-1924) to Edith Bolling Galt, who became his second wife

I do not know how to express or analyze the conflicting emotions that have surged like a storm through my heart (all night long). I only know that first and foremost in all my thoughts has been the glorious confirmation you gave me (last night) - without effort, unconsciously, as of course - of all I have ever thought of your mind and heart.

One could also begin the reading here:

You have the greatest soul, the noblest nature, the sweetest, most loving heart I have ever known, and my love, my reverence, my admiration for you, you have increased in one evening as I should have thought only a lifetime of intimate, loving association could have increased them.

You are more wonderful and lovely in my eyes than you ever were before; and my pride and joy and gratitude that you should love me with such a perfect love are beyond all expression, except in some great poem which I cannot write.

Parables & Fables
Readings #48 - #50

<u>Aesop's Fables: "The Lion in Love"</u>
A Lion once fell in love with a beautiful maiden. When the lion proposed marriage to her parents, they were at a loss. While they did not want to give her to the lion, they certainly didn't want him infuriated. After some consideration, the father offered this: "We are surely very honored by Your Majesty's proposal. However, our daughter is a delicate thing. We're afraid that in the fire of your passions, you could hurt her unwittingly. May we suggest that you have your claws and teeth extracted. This way, we would be happy to consider your proposal anew. The great lion was so in love, that he did have his claws removed and teeth taken out. Then, when he came to propose again to the parents of the maiden, they laughed right at him, no longer a threat. "Do your worst!"

Why this? Because love tames the fiercest of us all.

The First Woman in Nevada by Mark Twain

Old inhabitants tell how, in a certain Nevada camp, the news went abroad early in the morning that a woman was come! The miners had seen a calico dress hanging out of a wagon down at the camping ground---sign of emigrants from over the great plains. Everybody went down there, and a shout went up when an actual bona fide dress was discovered fluttering in the wind! The male emigrant was visible. The miners said:

"Fetch her out!"

He said: "It's my wife, gentlemen---she is sick---we have been robbed of money, provisions, everything, by the Indians---we want to rest."

"Fetch her out! We've got to see her!"

"But gentlemen, the poor thing, she---"

"FETCH HER OUT!"

He "fetched her out," and they swung their hats and sent up three rousing cheers, and they crowded around and gazed at her, and touched her dress, and listened to her voice with the look of men who listened to a memory rather than a present reality---and then they collected twenty-five hundreds dollars in gold and gave it to the man, and swung their hats again, and gave three more cheers, and went home satisfied.

Imagine an ending, added by the groom: *She must have looked like my beloved. I would pay just to look at her, too.*

<u>The Gift of the Magi, by O. Henry (very abridged)</u>

In this story, Della Young sets out to buy a gift for her beloved husband, Jim. They're very poor, but very much in love. Della mourns over what to get Jim, with so little money to spend. As she recovers, she notes her long beautiful, brown hair. She bundles up and heads out into the cold, to sell her hair for $20. Now she is able to find the perfect gift, an elegant chain for Jim's prized pocket watch.

At home, she tries to improve the looks of her now short hair and starts dinner.

When Jim arrives home, he's dumbfounded by her hair, and Della can't quite make out the meaning of his reaction. But when Jim presents Della with her present, he explains that she will understand.

She cries out in joy, then cries as she realizes; Jim had given her a set of expensive combs she had wanted for her hair, and did it by selling his prized pocket watch.

Truly, they are the wisest of everyone who gifts gifts. They are the magi. -

This story is typically one of Christmas; in which all assume the loving charm of the couple's sacrifice. But is the lesson to give until it hurts? Is it to sacrifice what you prize most? Or, could the lesson perhaps be, that you should do neither? Perhaps the lesson is that you should not give up the most valued parts of yourself in an attempt to please another, because in giving up yourself, neither of you wins after all.

This commentary offers a different interpretation, but something worth considering as marriage begins.

And 3 Surprise Extras
#51-#53

A Mashup of the wisdom of Francis of Assasi in one reading.

As Saint Francis of Assisi wrote, "All the darkness in the world cannot extinguish the light of a single candle. And, "A single sunbeam is enough to drive away many shadows."

May you be that candle and that sunbeam for one another, always.

And remember that, "When you leave this earth, you can take with you nothing that you have received, only what you have given."

So, may you not so much seek to be loved, as to love.

And give to each other this day, and forever more, your loyalty, your companionship, and your hearts, as we in your company give to you the same, and are now blessed, to witness this.

Compiled from, *Our Mutual Friend,* by Charles Dickens

"You know what I am going to say. I love you. What other men may mean when they use that expression, I cannot tell; what I mean is, that I am under the influence of some tremendous attraction which I have resisted in vain, and which overmasters me. You could draw me to fire, you could draw me to water, you could draw me to the gallows, you could draw me to any death, you could draw me to anything I have most avoided, you could draw me to any exposure and disgrace. This and the confusion of my thoughts, so that I am fit for nothing, is what I mean by your being the ruin of me. But if you would return a favourable answer to my offer of myself in marriage, you could draw me to any good--every good--with equal force."

"...Her heart — is given him, with all its love and truth. (She would joyfully die with him, or better than that, die for him.) She knows he has failings, but she thinks they have grown up through his being like one cast away, for the want of something to trust in, and care for, and think well of. ...And she says, that lady...only prove what a world of things I will do and bear for you..."

And for a classic but witty option,
a Mashup of some of Oscar Wilde's best wisdom.

"Most people are other people. Their thoughts are someone else's opinions, their lives a mimicry, their passions a quotation. So here, are more of Oscar Wilde's quotes...

"Men always want to be a woman's first love. That is their clumsy vanity. We women have a more subtle instinct about things. What we like is to be a man's last romance."

Remember...

"Women are meant to be loved, not to be understood."
And... "How can a woman be expected to be happy with a man who insists on treating her as if she were a perfectly normal human being?

So..."Keep love in your heart. A life without it is like a sunless garden when the flowers are dead. The consciousness of loving and being loved, brings warmth and richness to life that nothing else can bring."

In Closing...

Have fun with your reading. There are few rules you must absolutely follow, except for getting the approval of your Officiant ahead of time, certainly. Some religious services are still flexible, especially if you use a classic religious writer, or hymn lyric. In many other instances, it's up to you, your fiancé ...and your heart. So enjoy.

Heartfelt wishes for a wonderful wedding and marriage.

Disclaimer: The author(s) have made all reasonable efforts to present "50 Unique Wedding Readings " as an overview. A reasonable couple must review their readings with whomever serves as their legal wedding Officiant for legal and religious compliance. The author(s) assume no responsibility for any particular religious order's acceptance of the reader's wedding ceremony, or appropriateness of the reader's sense of humor, etc. when utilizing content for their ceremony.

Other books by Marie Kay:

50 New & Traditional Wedding Vow Examples
& How To Write Vows of Your Own: 10 Guides

Unique Wedding Ceremony Songs
& Where to Find Them

23126873R00043

Printed in Great Britain
by Amazon